Life's Coffee Notes

OrangeBooks Publication

Smriti Nagar, Bhilai, Chhattisgarh - 490020

Website: **www.orangebooks.in**

First Edition, 2023

LIFE'S COFFEE NOTES

A BLEND OF EXPERIENCES & WISDOM

Deepam Kanjani

OrangeBooks Publication

www.orangebooks.in

Life's Coffee Notes: A Blend of Experiences & Wisdom

-Deepam Kanjani

This book is a testament to the wisdom you've passed down to us Papa.

Deepam is a cyber-security architect and a speaker. His vivid, humorous, and thought-provoking musings on different perspectives of life, financial wizardry, and embracing adaptability have won him a place in the hearts and minds of a lot of people. He loves coffee and taking pictures.

In his first book, he's inviting you to join him on a unique journey as he spills the beans (or should we say, coffee beans? - well, literally too) on the vital principles that have steered his course – a voyage that began with a spark of curiosity in technology and led him to the creation of soul-stirring content that has touched lives across continents. What that really means is he has traveled the world - delivering workshops to a wide variety of audiences.

Deepam explores a kaleidoscope of life's hues, from the role of perspectives as your compass to success to the alchemy of prudent financial management. He delves into the beauty and growth found in our struggles and failures and uncovers the path to cultivating a heart of empathy. This isn't just a book; it's an invitation to a conversation, a debate, a late-night contemplation session under the stars. It's a collection of wisdom you'll find yourself returning to, like an old friend, time and time again. Read it when you think you need another perspective.

Deepam's hope? This book will be like a lantern, guiding you through the winding pathways of your own life journey, a source of inspiration, a blueprint for personal and professional growth, and maybe even a catalyst for a few hearty laughs along the way.

His blend of personal tales, quirky metaphors, and pragmatic guidance make this book more than just a read - it may be a life-altering experience, like a good cup of coffee on a rainy day. So here's an invitation to the most rewarding coffee date you'll ever have - Not literally, but if you know what I mean ;). Say yes, and you'll be taking the first step towards brewing a life that's as strong, balanced, and full-flavored as your favorite cup of coffee. So, are you ready to brew some life-changing insights?

DISCLAIMER

The book "Life's Coffee Notes: A Blend of Experiences & Wisdom" is a creative compilation of the author's experiences, perceptions, and observations gathered from various life scenarios and global explorations. It is written with the purpose of sharing knowledge, provoking thought, and promoting personal growth and is not intended to provide professional advice or a one-size-fits-all solution to any specific circumstance or challenge.

Names, locations, and identifying details of the individuals involved in the shared anecdotes have been altered to protect their privacy. Any resemblance to actual persons, living or dead, or actual events is purely coincidental. The stories and associated characters do not represent any person or event in reality, and any such correlation is unintended.

While every effort has been made to ensure the accuracy of the information in this book as of the publication date, the author and publisher do not assume and hereby disclaim any liability to any party for any loss, damage, or disruption caused by errors or omissions, whether such errors or omissions result from negligence, accident, or any other cause. The author and publisher are neither responsible for the results of any actions taken on the basis of the information in this work nor for any error in or omission from this work.

The book is intended to be read as an inspirational and motivational guide and does not purport to offer legal, financial, medical, or any other professional advice. If such advice or other expert assistance is needed, the services of a competent professional should be sought.

By reading this book, you agree that the author and company are not responsible for your success or failure resulting from any decisions you make related to any information presented in this book.

The content is solely the opinion of the author and is not intended to malign any religion, ethnic group, club, organization, company, or individual. The author disclaims any responsibility for any liability, loss, or risk, personal or otherwise, which is incurred as a consequence, directly or indirectly, of the use and application of any contents of this book.

INTRODUCTION

Picture this - there's always that one person you might have noticed in a cafe; engrossed in their laptop screen, their fingers dancing across the keyboard, they seem to be in their own world amidst the hum of frothing milk and the chitter-chatter around.

Their coffee - whether it's a creamy cappuccino or a strong espresso, sits beside them, steam swirling up from its surface as if it's the fuel propelling their focus.

Yet, ironically, if you were to ask them about the difference between their frothy cappuccino and rich espresso, they'd likely offer a blank stare.

As you read this, isn't there a face popping up in your mind, a smirk playing on your lips? Perhaps it's a friend, a colleague, or even a mirror image of you. Yes, I thought you might picture someone by now.

Well, this book may be just about knowing more about different kinds of coffees, and in the end, may just sound to be a bad decision because everything in this book is something you already know - directly or indirectly.

This book is not to reveal groundbreaking secrets or impart life lessons. The only purpose is to give you a gentle reminder of what and how life is outside of the cocoon we call "our world" - it's just a blend of my personal experiences, where life happens to all of us in similar yet the most unusual ways.

I am not going to claim that the book is going to change your perspective towards things or give you new insights towards life. Instead, it strives to put words to the thoughts that we all feel and thoughts that often go unexamined amidst the busyness of our lives.

You know what I mean!

One thing that my best friend keeps telling me: “Deepam, you can relate anything to anything.” Maybe that is what this book is - it relates Coffee to everything. My intention is just to make you more aware! This is only, so you can make choices from a place of consciousness rather than ignorance.

Within these pages, you will find a compilation of my thoughts, reflections, observations, and personal experiences that I had over the years traveling and having coffee. Nothing magical is going to happen here, just pick up a toast (if you like) and see life through the lens of a coffee enthusiast.

By sharing my experiences and insights in "Life’s Coffee Notes: A Blend of Experiences & Wisdom", my intention is just to guide you in your journey of self-enhancement. Let's embark on a journey of brewing a life brimming with strength, resilience, adaptability, continuous learning, balance, and sweetness.

The vision for "Life's Coffee Notes: A Blend of Experiences & Wisdom" is to weave an engaging, enlightening, and relatable guide for readers on their quest for self-improvement and personal growth. This book offers a metaphorical brew of life lessons, presented through the diverse aspects of coffee, with the objective to inspire, motivate, and guide individuals towards a deeper comprehension of themselves and the world.

Well, the next time you buy a coffee, ask the barista how they made it. The fun of it is always around the curiosity to learn. For ex: I did not know the importance of roasting beans at different temperatures would make such a huge difference.

Probably, it's just my overthinking and holding on to it that made me who I am.

Have a sip of coffee today.

ACKNOWLEDGEMENTS

The creation of this book has been built with love, a journey through time and space that has taken me from my birthplace to my college, workplace, and all the spaces in between.

I've drawn from a rich tapestry of experiences fueled by the interactions I've had and the lessons I've learned from the remarkable people I've met along the way with my anecdotes about coffee.

To begin with, I owe a wealth of gratitude to Cookie (a loving nickname that carries more affection than her real name ever could). As early as 2017, you've been my anchor in the ever-changing tides of life. We've shared laughter, tears, debates, and dreams, and through it all, you've been my constant. You're my safe haven, my grounding force, and your unwavering belief in me keeps me going.

To my sisters, Rashmi and Vandana, you've been my pillars of strength since I first tottered on tiny feet. Your love, guidance, and support have helped me navigate life's winding roads and challenging turns. You've been there during my ups and downs; steadfast and encouraging, your faith in me unshakable.

For my delightful nieces, who add joy and wonder to my life, know that I love you profoundly. Your infectious enthusiasm and zest for life constantly inspire me.

To my beloved parents, your love has been my compass; your faith in me is my foundation. The values you instilled in me have shaped the person I am today and continue to guide me in my journey.

A heartfelt thank you to my friends - the zany, inspiring bunch who always said, "You're a mad genius with a treasure chest of tales; let them out!" Your constant encouragement and faith in my storytelling abilities have played a pivotal role in the creation of this book.

I am grateful for the mentors who have guided me in both my professional and personal life.

Your wisdom and insights have enriched my understanding and perspective of the world.

And finally, a word of appreciation for those who doubted me. Your skepticism, ironically, fuelled my determination and spurred me on. You've taught me resilience, the art of proving oneself, and for that, I'm grateful.

Each of you has contributed a verse to the poem of my life, and this book is a reflection of that collective wisdom. Thank you for being a part of my journey.

Contents

PART – 1

ESPRESSO: THE STRONG BEGINNINGS

The fact that the book is based on coffee analogies implies that we will start with the first type of coffee – Espresso; it's concentrated and gives the strongest push to start the day. Much like how we need our days to begin with, setting up the basis of life-shaping perceptions, values and attitudes. This Part is dedicated to the understanding and cultivation of this vital trait.

Now, let's jog your memory a bit further. Ever had an alarm that didn't ring, but swayed? Allow me to explain.

Back in the day, my wake-up call wasn't the shrill beeping of an alarm clock. Oh no, it was a rhythmic thump-thump-thump seeping through the walls from my neighbor's place. You see, she taught an early morning Zumba class. The lively beats, the passionate yells, and the synchronous stomping all combined into a unique wake-up symphony.

And here's the interesting part - if the day's track list was to your liking, you'd find yourself grooving out of bed and your day kick-started with a dance. But, if the music wasn't quite your cup of tea, well, tough luck. The cacophony was just a rude awakening and a grumpy start to your day.

1) Importance of Roots

When we hear/read the word 'Espresso'- the first impression is our senses reminding us of a bitter black concentrated drink. What people do not know is that its taste is determined by the quality of its beans.

It is cherished worldwide for its full-bodied flavor and energizing qualities. Similarly, in the journey of life, our foundation is built on resilience - the strength to persist and endure challenging situations. Likewise, our beginnings and roots play a very important role in the person we grow up to be. Usually, this is influenced heavily by our cultural values - what we see at home and what we learn at school - this is our original flavor, our core essence.

"Just as the flavor of the espresso is influenced by the quality of its beans, our essence is molded by our origins and cultural values."

What if our roots aren't perfect? What if we come from difficult circumstances, or what if we don't have a home or parents or have a rocky start?

The good news is that just like a skilled barista can make a world-class espresso with average beans, we, too, can transcend our beginnings and make a wonderful future.

Choose how you want to be the same, and the world will push you towards it.

The **first step is to acknowledge your past without letting it define your future.** I know this is something that you would've heard many times. Think of it like holding your past like shackles, not letting you move forward. But if you learn from it and its influence, you are good to understand and to make a conscious effort to build on positives and learn from negatives.

Transport yourself back with me for a moment, to the good old days of after-school tuition sessions.

Picture this - a delightful lady with silver hair, wielding a cane, not out of necessity but more like a prop. She was my tuition teacher, a veritable fountain of knowledge and wisdom. A music lover at heart, she savored melodies from golden oldies of Bollywood, the kind of tunes that waft through the air and pull at your heartstrings. But her real passion was education, and it wasn't constrained by chalk and blackboard, desks and benches. Instead, she believed in turning every corner of life into a classroom, every situation into a lesson.

Every day after school, I would trudge along the familiar path leading to her warm, inviting house. She had a huge backyard. The house was more than just a tuition class; it was a treasure trove of knowledge and wisdom.

Back then, I wouldn't feel it that way ;)

If you happened to be late, she had a unique form of 'punishment'. She would direct you to go and stand in the garden while memorizing solutions. The summers there were intense. The heat would waft through the air, the sun a golden orb dominating the azure sky, pouring warmth onto the earth below. Each minute in that summer sun felt like an hour. It was during those scorching moments, with beads of sweat trickling down my forehead and the relentless sun glaring down upon me; the lesson sank in that time is valuable, and respecting it was paramount. The hotter it was, the faster the lesson would get memorized.

This form of punishment wasn't about making us uncomfortable; it was about teaching us to value time and commitment. Every uncomfortable minute under the sun, I'd resolve to be punctual and to respect not just my own time but also that of others. It was not a punishment but an impactful lesson disguised in the garb of one. It was a kind of reinforcement to do good and better.

In retrospect, the garden was more than just a space for reflection; it was a metaphor for life.

Just as the garden endured the harsh summer sun to bloom into magnificence, we, too, had to bear the hardships and challenges of life to evolve into better individuals. This was her teaching – an innovative approach to imbibing life skills along with academic ones. And just like the garden that bloomed vibrantly despite the adversities, her lessons have stayed with me, guiding me through the seasons of my life, including today.

Just as the roots of a tree are vital for its growth, survival, and flourishing, the lessons imparted by her were the roots of our personal and academic development. She sowed the seeds of punctuality, respect, and commitment in our hearts, watered them with her wisdom, and nurtured them under the sun of adversity.

In conclusion, our roots - the lessons and values we imbibe early in life - define our actions and shape our futures. They ground us in our beliefs and help us stand firm in the face of adversities, just as a tree stands tall and strong, anchored by its deep, nourishing roots.

"Our roots sculpt our actions, shape our future, and fortify our resilience."

Reflection point: Think about your roots. How have they shaped you? What can you learn from your past, and how can you use these insights to shape your future?

2) Overcoming Challenges

Like any strong coffee – the espresso shot goes through immense pressure during brewing, transforming from simple water and coffee grounds into a complex, flavorful beverage. Similarly, life puts a lot of pressure- it's during these moments of difficulty, these challenges, where the real transformation happens.

Every one of us encounters obstacles, disappointments, and failures. They are intrinsic elements of our journey. The secret isn't to evade these moments, but to master the art of overcoming them, to metamorphose under pressure, akin to the process of brewing espresso. Bear in mind, the nature of your outcome, be it bitter or rich in flavor, is contingent on how you handle adversity, just as the taste of an espresso hinges on its interaction with temperature and pressure.

One thing that we can learn from Espresso is to develop resilience to pressure in a way - Once you start doing the same, it trickles the perception of failure. Instead of seeing it as a negative end, view it as an opportunity for growth, a stepping stone to success.

"Pressure fuels excellence, shaping strength in adversity."

Remember, no espresso is made without pressure.

Reflection point: Recall a recent setback or challenge you faced. How did you react to it? What did it teach you, and how can you use this learning to grow stronger?

Let me share with you another story that underscores the importance of resilience. The year was 2007. On a chilly winter evening in Delhi, I was blanketed in a heavy fog, served as the backdrop. I was scheduled to take an overnight train from Delhi to Bhopal, a city in the heart of India, Madhya Pradesh. With the fog reducing visibility to nearly zero, even a minor delay could disrupt my planned journey (might miss the train).

My journey to the railway station involved multiple modes of transport starting from a shared rickshaw from my accommodation, a city bus, and finally another rickshaw to the station. I had to leave at 4 in the evening for the train that was at 9 pm, just to accommodate any unexpected delays.

As I began my journey, I met an elderly woman, frail and struggling to walk in the biting cold and treacherous fog. As fate would have it, our paths were intertwined as she needed assistance reaching a location that lay on my route. A small voice in my head fretted about the potential delay, the nagging worry about missing my train growing louder. But the foggy evening, the lady's vulnerability, and my conscience didn't allow me to ignore her plea.

Choosing kindness over convenience, I decided to help her. The journey took longer than expected, and as I bid her goodbye and headed for the station, I had already accepted the possibility of missing my train.

However, destiny had a surprise in store. My train was delayed due to the intense fog; the very factor that I thought would make me miss it. Not only did I board the train on time, but the ticket collector offered me an upgrade to a better coach. A family wanted to travel together, and my willingness to switch gave them that opportunity while providing me with a more comfortable journey.

Reflecting on this, I realized this wasn't merely a fortunate coincidence. It was a life lesson beautifully disguised as a travel anecdote. The act of kindness, done without any expectation, didn't just protect me but unexpectedly rewarded me in the most unexpected manner.

In the end, it wasn't the fog, the journey, or the potential delay that defined that winter evening. It was resilience – the resilience to make the right choice even when it wasn't the most convenient one, the resilience to persist even when the odds seemed stacked against me, and the resilience to maintain a positive attitude amidst uncertainty.

Coming back to the potent shot of Espresso that powers us through the day, resilience powers us through life. It allows us to endure and bounce back from difficulties, making our journey not just possible but meaningful too.

In another instance, while I was staying in Manila on a short-term work assignment. I once had the privilege of meeting this lovely elderly woman Mrs. Tan with more life stories than the many products she sold in her little grocery store. One fine evening, as I was browsing through the aisles of her shop, she saw me stressed and invited me to narrate a tale that carried a potent life lesson.

Mrs. Tan introduced me to the concept of 'crab mentality', using an analogy that has stayed with me. If you put crabs in a bowl, she began, and one tried to climb to freedom, the others would pull it back down. It's an 'if I can't have it, neither can you' kind of thinking. At first glance, it might seem like a straightforward commentary on the crabs' behavior. Until this point, my patience was very low as I started losing interest, but she took the narrative a step further.

"Do crabs naturally belong in a bowl?" She asked with a twinkle in her eye. The answer, of course, was “No”. Crabs are creatures of the ocean, not confined glass bowls. Someone, she explained, had exercised their power and control to trap the crabs in a restricted, unnatural state. This, she suggested, was akin to what happens when those in power force less fortunate ones to scramble for their livelihoods, creating an environment where they feel compelled to bring each other down to survive, which suddenly started making a lot of sense to me.

The real lesson, she conveyed, was not about the crabs' behavior but the circumstances that led to it. The crabs weren't inherently selfish or destructive; they were victims of their circumstances but struggling to survive. And much like the crabs, people, too, when placed in constrained conditions, may act out in ways that don't reflect their natural character.

But the narrative needn't end there. She, despite her humble lifestyle and meager resources, was a living testament to the power of resilience and learning from setbacks. With every hardship she faced, she learned, grew, and found ways to break free from her own 'bowl,' refusing to succumb to the 'crab mentality.' She took control of her circumstances, determined not to let adversity define her actions or beliefs.

All she told me towards the end was not to judge those who seem trapped in their own bowls, struggling to break free, but rather to understand their circumstances and help create an environment where they can flourish naturally. It was a short yet meaningful way to get my mind untangled. As we navigate our lives, it is crucial to be mindful of the bowls we may unknowingly be placed in and strive to break free, to grow beyond constraints, and to never allow setbacks to dictate our potential for growth. This also includes being judgment free for people in the 'bowl'.

Let's take a 'Coffee Break':

Brewing Resilience Exercise:

- ✓ Write down three challenges you've faced in the past.
- ✓ Next, jot down what you learned from each of these experiences.
- ✓ Finally, write how these learning have helped you or can help you in the future.

This is the essence of our 'Espresso' Part: acknowledging our roots and transforming challenges into stepping stones towards personal growth. And remember, just like espresso, it's not about where or how you start but the flavor you bring to the world. In the next Part, 'Americano: Worldly Brews', we'll explore how being adaptable can help us navigate life's ever-changing landscapes.

PART 2

AMERICANO: WORLDLY BREWS

While Americano is nothing but espresso diluted with hot water, making it less intense yet rich in flavor - adapting and stretching its robust essence into a milder and versatile beverage; similarly, life requires us to adapt to new situations and environments. This Part is about exploring adaptability and how it influences our experiences.

Much like an Americano, stepping out into the world and experiencing different cultures can dilute our rigid beliefs and make our understanding richer and more nuanced.

"Embrace the tapestry of culture and diversity, for in the clarity of understanding, your thoughts ignite and your growth finds fuel."

Traveling the world and meeting with people may or may not be the best thing in the world, but it definitely enriches your thought process.

1) Broadening Perspectives

Just as adding water to an espresso creates an Americano, exposing ourselves to diverse cultures, societies, and beliefs expands our horizons.

Travel, even if it's just to a different city or town in your own country, can bring new perspectives. In India, people travel to explore horizons from mountains to oceans, from spices to chocolates, from teas to coffee, from Tollywood to Hollywood - it's like a power pack of different understandings and angles that make us appreciate the value of diversity.

But it's not just about physical travel- sometimes your Kindle, Netflix on your machine or even conversations with people from different backgrounds can also broaden your perspective, your mind and your story. The more you learn about the world, the more you adapt and become flexible and able to navigate life's twists and turns with ease.

If I would ask for water to drink - people in most developed nations would point me towards the tap, but the same might be extremely estranged for others.

My first trip to Germany, fresh out of college and newly plunged into the professional world, offered me a lesson in adaptability that I still hold dear. I was staying in Essen, a small town known to be the energy capital of Germany, far from the familiar comforts of home - India.

One winter evening, feeling extremely hungry, I stumbled upon a small, cozy pizza place near Grugapark in Essen. The waitress, a kind-hearted woman, couldn't speak a word of English. I, on the other hand, had no knowledge of German. As I stood shivering in the cold outside the restaurant, she stepped out to understand what I was looking for.

Through a hilariously memorable fifteen-minute sign language conversation, I tried to convey my dietary preference - vegetarian. I enacted various vegetables, trying to differentiate them from meat; all the while, the waitress watched me with an amused expression.

Eventually, she understood, or at least seemed to, and went in to get something to eat.

She returned with a slice of Margherita pizza and a Coke and asked for 5 euros in exchange. Despite the language barrier and cultural differences, her patience and dedication to helping me were commendable. Her gestures transcended the limitations of language and culture, offering me a warm, much-needed sense of familiarity in that foreign land.

Over the next few weeks, this pizza place became my regular dining spot. The waitress would get something different yet vegetarian for me each evening, and we'd share laughs over my continued attempts to explain the concept of vegetarianism using pantomime.

This bond we formed, despite the language barrier and cultural differences, became a symbol of human connection and adaptability for me. I learned that cultural differences are not barriers but bridges to new experiences, understanding, and bonds.

Reflection Point: Reflect on an experience where encountering a different culture or perspective changed your viewpoint or attitude. How did it impact your understanding of the world?

2) Cultivating Adaptability

An Americano can be enjoyed hot or iced, showcasing its adaptability. In life, being adaptable is not about changing who you are but about adjusting your approach depending on the situation.

Cultivating adaptability starts with being open-minded, willing to learn, and embracing change. Whether it's adjusting to a new job, relocating to a new city, or dealing with unexpected life events, adaptability is a skill that can help you thrive in any circumstance. Remember adaptability is not a factor of resilience. It defines your capacity to be flexible to "change", which is inevitable.

Adapting to a new culture, just like getting accustomed to a new coffee flavor, might seem challenging initially. But once you cross that initial hurdle, it enriches your life, making it more colorful and diverse. It's like navigating an ocean - the first wave may seem intimidating, but once you learn to ride it, you can sail with the breeze.

In my college days, there was a hawker's corner in Noida known for serving their unique dish called "Honey Chilli Potatoes topped with Sesame Seeds" aka HCPs. My friends and I frequented the place, seeking respite from the mundane hostel food. The hawker's stall always had a long line of eager customers, patiently waiting for the perfect momos and the delightful honey chilli potatoes. It wasn't just a place to grab a quick bite; it was a vibrant hub where students worked on assignments, artists found inspiration, friends caught up, and even business meetings took place. It had become a true community hub.

One fateful day, a citywide power outage struck, plunging the entire block into darkness, including the hawker's stall. What was once a lively atmosphere turned into confusion and silence. The cooking pans went quiet, and the comforting warmth of the ovens faded away. Everyone, including the hawkers, was concerned, as they were unprepared for such a situation.

Yet, there was a symbiotic relationship between the customers and the hawkers. The customers relied on them for nourishment, while the hawkers depended on their patronage for their livelihood. In the face of this unexpected challenge, a group of students stepped up. They provided small battery-powered lights, power banks and placed candles on every table, creating a warm and intimate ambiance. Though it was far from the usual experience, the taste of the food remained as amazing as ever.

Word spread about the situation, reaching nearby offices and colleges. The place became famous for its candle-lit momos, HCPs and coffee. The community found solace and comfort in the sense of normalcy they had collectively managed to create amidst the chaos. What could have been a disaster for the hawker's business became an unforgettable and heartwarming experience for the customers, a testament to their resilience.

When the city's power was finally restored, and the place was once again bathed in light, the hawkers looked around with smiles on their faces. They realized that the power outage had not only taught them the importance of adaptability but also solidified their place in the community. Their stalls somehow had become a symbol of strength, unity, and the indomitable spirit that can transform challenges into opportunities.

This story reminds us that even in the darkest times when faced with unexpected obstacles, our collective resilience and willingness to support one another can illuminate the path forward. It is through such challenges that we discover the true essence of community and find the strength to overcome adversity, leaving an indelible mark on our lives and the world around us.

Nothing new from the excerpt; we can see that life often throws unexpected challenges our way. The key lies in not being rigid and resistant to change but in being adaptable, finding alternative solutions, and making the best of the situation. It teaches us that even in the face of adversity, our ability to adapt can turn a setback into an opportunity. Whether it's a power outage at a popular cafe or a personal challenge, cultivating adaptability is what helps us persevere and ultimately thrive.

Reflection Point: Can you recall a time when you had to adapt quickly to an unexpected situation? What did it teach you? How has it shaped your approach to similar situations since?

Let's take a 'Coffee Break': Worldly Brews Exercise:

- ✓ Write down three things you have learned from other cultures or experiences.
- ✓ Next to each, write how this knowledge has changed your outlook or behavior.
- ✓ Finally, consider how you can further broaden your perspective. List three actions you can take to expose yourself to new ideas or cultures.

Just like the versatile Americano, embracing diversity and cultivating adaptability can help us navigate life's complexities with grace. As we move on to our next Part, 'Macchiato: Coded Layers', we'll delve into the importance of patience, problem-solving, and lifelong learning in mastering life's intricacies.

PART 3

MACCHIATO: CODED LAYERS

The next coffee is an espresso with a small amount of frothed milk. The blend creates layers - a strong espresso base with a touch of smoothness from the milk. This Part, akin to a Macchiato, signifies how our life is layered with various challenges and learning experiences, and with the strong base being the art of patience and problem-solving, the frothy layer symbolizing continuous learning and adaptation.

1) The Art of Patience and Problem-Solving

In making a Macchiato, the espresso must be brewed first, signifying the importance of a strong foundation in life. Just like when your apartment is getting constructed, the foundation takes the most time as it has to be the strongest as it analogically refers to life; this foundation is often patience and the ability to solve problems.

Patience is a virtue that guides us through trying times and keeps us grounded in moments of success. It's the power to endure, to wait for the right moment, and to persist when results are not immediate.

Problem-solving, on the other hand, is the ability to identify and overcome obstacles effectively. It's about employing logic, creativity, and insight to find solutions, a skill crucial not just in work but in all areas of life.

"Patience ignites the mind to meaningful solutions."

Do we know and have enough of it?

In the enchanting city of Johor Bahru, Malaysia, where cultural richness intertwines with modernity, I encountered a wise old man Mr. Percy who ran a beloved roadside stall selling 'kuey teow,' a renowned local noodle dish. Little did I know the cultural adventure that awaited me.

Amidst the charm of this bustling city, a major roadwork project was announced, threatening the livelihoods of the shop owners, including Mr. Percy's noodle stall. Dust-filled surroundings and the noisy construction disrupted the once vibrant food scene.

However, amidst the chaos, a few remarkable individuals chose a different path. They embraced the power of patience, understanding the necessity of the roadwork for the city's development. Instead of succumbing to frustration, they unleashed their problem-solving prowess.

With the assistance of the local association, they relocated to a nearby parking area, creating a clean and convenient pathway for customers to reach their cherished food stalls. Temporary screens were erected, shielding them from the dust's intrusion. Surprisingly, even the workers involved in the road work began patronizing these stalls, uniting the community through their shared meals.

Every morning, these resilient vendors, led by Mr. Percy, would gather their unwavering patience and problem-solving skills shining through. Their positive spirit, coupled with the irresistible aroma of 'kuey teow,' continued to draw customers, defying the challenges imposed by the ongoing construction.

What could have been a disaster transformed into a testament to the power of patience and problem-solving? This story serves as a poignant reminder that life will inevitably present roadblocks, but with patience, creative thinking, and a resilient mindset, we can possess the ability to overcome any hurdle, emerging even stronger than before.

While the fact that Mr. Percy's willingness, composure and patience prove to be a strong motivation point. It also tells us about how our life is filled with moments of haste and a little bit of light; direction and patience are all we need to clear the fog.

Reflection Point: Consider a situation where your patience was tested. How did you respond? Similarly, recall an instance where you successfully solved a problem. What approach did you use, and what did it teach you?

2) Staying Updated: The Frothy Layer

The layer of frothed milk in a Macchiato signifies the continuous learning and updating that tops off our strong foundation. In an ever-evolving world, staying updated, learning new skills, and broadening our knowledge base is no longer optional; it's a necessity.

Continuous learning helps us stay relevant, adaptable, and forward-thinking. It keeps us engaged, promotes creativity, and enhances our problem-solving skills.

"Knowledge propels our journey through life."

Reflection Point: What are you doing to ensure continuous learning? How has it benefited you in your personal or professional life?

Let's talk of another story - My quest for a Paying Guest accommodation in Singapore landed me in the house of a thoughtful landlady, who became an unexpected source of learning and growth for me. Her uncanny ability to decode my problems and provide innovative solutions was nothing short of an inspiration.

I recall the day when homesickness loomed over me like a dark cloud, robbing me of my usual spirits. Sensing my low mood, my landlady surprised me by preparing an Indian curry. The familiar aroma instantly lifted my spirits, making me feel a little less far away from home. This act taught me about the power of empathy and cultural sensitivity, and how these traits could touch lives in profound ways.

In another instance, she took my clothes out of the dryer and got them ironed when I forgot. This seemingly small act of kindness highlighted the importance of responsibility and attention to detail. It taught me how small acts could make a significant difference, a lesson that I have since applied in my professional and personal life.

However, my learning didn't stop within the confines of my accommodation. Every time I stepped out, I found lessons waiting to be learned. I remember seeing a child who yearned for a school but couldn't afford it.

The sight of his parents trying their best to provide for his education served as a stark reminder of the value of resilience, determination, and the transformative power of education.

Then there was the waiter at a café who worked tirelessly, saving every bit to buy a gift for his son. Despite being able to afford a S$20 coffee, many patrons hesitated to leave a S$2 tip. This made me reflect upon our responsibilities towards one another and the need to extend our generosity to those who could benefit from it.

The essence of life, much like a Macchiato, is not confined to a single element. It's a blend of experiences, interactions, observations, and continuous learning. Every person we meet and every situation we encounter presents an opportunity to learn, adapt, and grow. We just need to be receptive and open-minded.

Remember, learning isn't a destination; it's a lifelong journey. And every step on this journey takes us closer to becoming a better version of ourselves. In the next Part,

'Cappuccino: Blending Finances', we'll discuss the importance of financial stability and how it contributes to personal growth and security.

PART 4

CAPPUCCINO: BLENDING FINANCES

EVery time you pass by a train station or any known food court - the most popular coffee beverage is a harmonious blend of equal parts of espresso, steamed milk, and froth - Cappuccino. Life, like a perfectly crafted Cappuccino, thrives on balance, and it is our job to maintain that balance. In this Part, we will explore the balance in financial life, the lessons I learned from personal experience, and how you can apply these insights to your life.

1) Financial Literacy: The Espresso Base

Financial literacy forms a strong base, much like the espresso in a Cappuccino. For instance, knowing how much tax you are paying and what doesn't make all the difference but knowing how to manage, invest and save money will help strategize taxes more efficiently. The expectation is not for every next person to become a financial wizard, but it is important to know the basics well enough to make informed decisions.

Financial literacy gives you the freedom - to be self-reliant; it opens up opportunities, and most importantly, it gives you the confidence to take control of your money.

"Financial literacy is the key that unlocks a world of financial freedom and adventure."

During my time in Dubai, a city known for its glitz, I met a hardworking car-driving instructor - Ahmed. Originally from India, he had moved to Dubai with the dream of creating a better life for his family back home.

His infectious energy and warm smile made every student feel welcome.

One day, as we cruised past the towering skyscrapers, Ahmed shared his story. He had been in Dubai for over a decade, working diligently and sending almost every dirham he earned back home. But despite his hard work and sacrifice, he lamented that he was struggling to make any real financial progress.

Intrigued and empathetic, I asked him more about his financial habits. It turned out that he had never been given any formal education on managing money. He was excellent at saving but had no understanding of concepts like investing, inflation, or financial planning. His hard-earned money sat idle in a basic savings account, making no real growth over the years.

I spent the next few weeks as a part of my driving classes sharing basic financial principles with him. We discussed the importance of budgeting, the concept of inflation, and the power of compound interest. I introduced him to safe investment options available for expats in Dubai and taught him how to diversify his earnings to create a balanced portfolio.

Over time, he took these lessons to heart. He started to save strategically, setting aside a portion of his earnings for different goals - his family's immediate needs, his children's education, and his own retirement. He also began to invest a portion of his income, understanding that while it carried some risk, it was also the key to growing his wealth over time.

While I did not get my license test cleared, he kept encouraging me to retry and told me that he was about to leave for India in a few months.

Fast forward a few months when I was about to leave Dubai, I got a call from an unknown number - It was Ahmed. He was a changed man. He talked excitedly about his investment plans, dreams for his family's future, and the dreams that now seemed much more achievable. He was in India and had saved enough with vested investments to buy land in India that he would go and use for agricultural purposes.

Ahmed's story is a powerful testament to the importance of financial literacy. It is not about how much money you make but how well you can manage and grow that money. With the right knowledge and understanding, anyone, from taxi drivers to office workers, can take control of their financial future. His journey underscores the transformative power of financial literacy and its potential to change lives, even in the glittering cityscape of Dubai.

Reflection Point: How would you rate your financial literacy on a scale of 1-10? What steps can you take to improve it? For instance, do you know exactly at this moment - how much tax you would have to pay this Financial Year? If not, then you need to learn more!

2) Building Financial Stability: The Milk and Froth

Just as the milk and froth balance out the intense espresso, savings and investments balance out your spending, leading to financial stability.

Savings act as a safety net, giving you peace of mind during unforeseen circumstances, while investing is a way to grow your wealth over time. It's all about making your money work for you, ensuring you're not just living paycheck to paycheck.

"It is always easy to save money than making more money for most individuals."

My initial days in a corporate job in Bangalore were fraught with financial difficulties. My monthly income was quickly consumed by medical expenses (25%), amenities such as rent and loans (40%), commuting and travel (10%), and unforeseen contingencies (10%); the remaining chunk disappeared into the inevitable black hole of taxes. Savings? They stood at a stark zero.

By the fifth day of each month, I would often find myself skimming the surface of debt. Some months, unexpected expenses would push me even deeper, accelerating the accumulation of debt and creating an ever-increasing sense of instability. However, amid this challenging phase, I was fortunate to have the support of people who helped during these tough times. Their kindness and generosity are something I will forever be grateful for.

The recurring cycle of financial instability made me realize the dire need for a robust financial plan. It wasn't an overnight transformation but a gradual and consistent process.

Let me give you my rule, though that might not be the most ideal, it is fairly simple to generalize in the first place:

25-25-25-25

- ✓ 25 - Pay Off High-Interest Debts
- ✓ 25 - Establish an Emergency Fund
- ✓ 25 - Secure Your Health and Invest in Future
- ✓ 25 - Pay off your amenities (Live Within Your Means)

Does that mean that with my paycheck increasing every year by a small percentage, should this remain the same?

Well, No. Don't let your salary hikes dictate your lifestyle. Instead, invest wisely to ensure a comfortable future, even when your body can no longer earn. Embrace the wisdom of those who live for the present, for what if you could do the same?

"Embrace the present, but always plan for what lies ahead."

Do I have what it takes to attain financial freedom?

No.

Does it mean I know how to create a balance in my financial life?

No.

But I know what it means not to have one, and I am grateful for the lessons that hardship taught me. Remember, financial stability is not solely about your earnings but about how effectively you manage your income and expenses.

Reflection Point: What steps are you taking to save and invest your money? Are your current financial habits leading you towards financial stability?

Let's take a 'Coffee Break':

Blending Finances Exercise:

- ✓ Jot down your current financial habits - Your income, spending, saving, and investing patterns.
- ✓ Identify areas where you could make improvements and set actionable goals for each.
- ✓ Develop a realistic financial plan for the next year and review it regularly to stay on track.

Remember, achieving financial stability doesn't happen overnight. It requires knowledge, discipline, and patience. But once you attain it, it contributes significantly to your overall well-being and personal growth.

In the next Part, 'Latte: The Comfort of Relationships'. We will delve into the importance of relationships in our lives, and how nurturing them contributes to our happiness and overall well-being.

PART 5

LATTE: THE COMFORT OF RELATIONSHIPS

A Latte is the perfect harmony of strong espresso and smooth steamed milk, topped with a little froth. It represents consistency in pattern, much like the one we need between reality and our perceptions. In this Part, we'll discuss how our perspective can shape our reality and how changing this perspective can lead to growth and transformation.

"The bridge between reality and perceptions reveals the transformative power of our perspectives."

My first exposure to a Latte happened to coincide with a situation that taught me the power of words and perspectives. I was sitting in a cafe in Frankfurt, savoring a latte while preparing for a critical presentation the next day. I was confused, battling with my nerves when I heard a conversation at the next table. A father-son conversation where the father explained to his son how perception could change the whole narrative.

The father said, "Think about it. When you say, 'I have to go to study,' it sounds like a chore. But when you say, 'I get to go to study,' it sounds like an opportunity. The situation hasn't changed, but your perspective has."

Hearing this conversation had a profound impact on me. It shook me and made me reframe my thoughts from "I have to present tomorrow" to "I get to present tomorrow." This slight change turned my nervousness into excitement, and my worry into anticipation.

In the following years, all of it started to come together because I had a similar conversation in school where one of my English teachers kept saying there is immense power in 'words & frames'. I learned that our perspective could shape our reality. She used to encourage me to go participate in Elocution competitions which led to a boost in confidence.

Taking another example - At the time, when I was asked to lead a team that had a reputation for being underperformers. Initially, I perceived it as a punishment, but then I chose to see it as an opportunity to motivate, guide, and bring out the best in this team. Within a few weeks, our 'underperforming' team had become one of the most successful ones in our organization. We made an app that delivered a $5M+ impact within sixty days of its launch.

It's just reflecting on the simplicity that surrounds us. It dawns upon us that in the hustle and bustle of our lives, we often complicate things. We chase after possessions, titles, and achievements, forgetting that true happiness often lies in the simplest of things.

This kind of built a small poem -

Experiences or possessions, what's the toll?

Clutter or mountains, what fills the soul?

Quality over quantity, the mindful role,

Accepting change is the ultimate goal.

Let us talk about another story - Several years ago, I found myself nervously pacing the hallways of the U.S. Embassy in Singapore, waiting for my B1 visa interview. In my hands, I held a file brimming with documents - financial statements, proof of employment.

But despite all my preparations, I was consumed by a bundle of nerves. There is a queue outside where people are supposed to wait for their time to appear for interviews. I was anxious to hear stories of people getting rejections. While I was practicing some last-minute responses, another applicant noticed my anxiety.

This person said, "Remember, it's not just about what you say in the interview; it's also about how you say it. Clear, confident communication can make all the difference."

His advice resonated with me, and I realized that my fear was hindering my ability to communicate effectively. I had all the necessary documents and qualifications, but unless I could express myself confidently and coherently, I might stumble. And most importantly, all my documents and reasoning were in order.

I prepared not just to answer the questions but also to engage in a meaningful dialogue with the visa officer.

When the time came for the interview, I was ready. I confidently answered the officer's questions, communicated my intentions for the trip clearly, and responded with sincerity. My preparation paid off, and I was granted the visa.

Even the most prepared and qualified individuals can falter if they cannot communicate their thoughts and intentions clearly. Whether it's a visa interview, a job interview, or any other high-stakes situation, strong communication skills are often the key to making a positive impression and achieving the desired outcome.

Reflection Point: Reflect on your communication skills. How well do you express yourself? Are you a good listener? How can you improve?

Imagine this - You're waiting in line at a local coffee shop, and a man cuts in front of you. Annoyed, you tap his shoulder to point out that he skipped the queue. He turns around with a surprised expression, apologizes and steps back.

You couldn't help but think: Why would he cut the line in the first place?

Initially, you were frustrated by his thoughtless act, but then you tried to see the situation from his perspective. Was he in a rush?

Did he not notice the queue? Perhaps he was preoccupied with his thoughts?

In an attempt to see his point of view, you started to consider factors that you might not have thought about initially. Perhaps he had a pressing issue or was late for an important meeting. Or maybe, he was just not a morning person and hadn't had his coffee yet.

By understanding the possible reasons behind his actions, your initial frustration subsided. The incident was a reminder that before judging or reacting to someone's action, it's essential to try and understand their perspective. It's all too easy to assume the worst in people, but sometimes, taking a step back and looking at the situation through their lens can change how we respond to the situation.

Though it's a simple everyday encounter, it left an impactful lesson about empathy and understanding. It's not about endorsing wrong actions but about considering the bigger picture. After all, everyone is fighting their own battles that we know nothing about.

Reflection Point: Think about a recent disagreement you had with someone. Can you understand their perspective? How could seeing their point of view change your approach to the situation?

Let's take a 'Coffee Break':

Words & Frames Exercise:

- ✓ Identify three situations where you could have communicated more effectively. What could you have done differently?

- ✓ List down three disagreements or misunderstandings you had due to differing perspectives. How could understanding the other person's viewpoint have changed the outcome?
- ✓ Develop actionable strategies to improve your communication skills and ability to understand different perspectives.

In life, as in a Latte, the blend of strong expressions and understanding creates a satisfying experience. In the next Part, 'Affogato: Sweet Life Lessons', we will delve into how to navigate through our emotions, the importance of emotional resilience, and how our emotions are a crucial part of our journey towards personal growth.

PART 6

AFFOGATO: SWEET LIFE LESSONS

Affogato, an Italian coffee-based dessert, is a delightful mix of vanilla gelato 'drowned' with a shot of hot espresso. It symbolizes the blend of sweet and bitter moments, teaching us to savor life lessons drawn from both. In this Part, we will explore how embracing challenges and learning from them help our personal growth.

"Embrace challenges as stepping stones, for within them lay the opportunity to learn, grow, and unleash your full potential."

So far, you already know that there is an incoming story - A few years ago, I was entrusted with leading a cyber-security project for a significant client. The journey was much like savoring an Affogato - a blend of sweet victories and bitter challenges. The project was a multi-million dollar transformation project.

Halfway through the project, we faced a setback - the client refused to complete the project due to financial constraints.

Through days and nights of relentless work, we managed to contain the situation - we started with cost-cutting, effective automation, and reducing operational costs by one-fourth of the proposed value. The relief and accomplishment that followed were as sweet as a spoonful of vanilla gelato. This experience taught me invaluable lessons about leadership, crisis management, personal resilience, and most importantly, the value of perseverance.

Now let me sprinkle some cocoa on our Affogato with another slice of life.

As a cyber-security architect, I often found myself in the need of justifying my decisions and actions. Our job is to protect, but to some, it may seem that we are hindering progress due to the added layers of security, much like how a child may see a parent as an obstacle to setting boundaries for safety.

In an interesting conversation with one of my peers - he brought up an interesting personal life story - "One day, I came home and decided to surprise my wife by taking over her usual chore of boiling milk. But instead of being pleasantly surprised, she raised a skeptical eyebrow, "Why today? Why haven't you done this before?" Her doubt echoed the same suspicions I face at work."

These scenarios, though distinct, had a common thread – the intent behind actions and decisions was often misunderstood or questioned. However, the key lies in knowing and staying true to your intent. If you have a larger purpose in mind, whether it's protecting a client's digital assets, assisting your spouse at home, or educating your child, standing firm amidst doubts will only make you stronger.

Sweet or bitter, life will continue to serve us Affogato moments. Our resilience lies in how we savor these experiences, extract the learnings, and continue to grow.

I remember reading this somewhere, "Our resilience is like a spicy salsa recipe: we savor life's experiences, extract the learnings, and keep adding that extra kick of growth."

Reflection Point: Think about your recent highs and lows. What have they taught you? How have they shaped your current situation or outlook on life?

In the heart of Manchester, I found myself sharing an apartment with Max. Max was an Equity trader. His daily routine was a dizzying blur of stock market figures, endless meetings, and late-night work sessions. Sleep was a luxury, and personal time, a distant dream.

His life's pendulum seemed to swing wildly towards work, leaving little room for anything else. Over the months, the once enthusiastic and vibrant Max began to lose his spark. His energy levels dwindled, and his smiles became rare. It seemed like he was constantly chasing after time, trapped in a relentless work cycle.

One summer evening, I noticed him sitting on our balcony, a blank look on his face as he stared out at the city's skyline. Joining him, I suggested a simple idea - a weekend getaway. No work, no calls, just us and the peaceful serenity of the countryside.

Initially resistant, Max eventually agreed; he signed off on a much-needed break. Nestled in the tranquility of nature, away from the buzz of the city, we started discussing the concept of balance.

He eventually just went on a weekend getaway. Upon returning, Max incorporated changes into his lifestyle. He started going for morning runs and dedicated time to reading. He learned to switch off from work at the end of the day, making time to unwind and rejuvenate. He found his balance.

The transformation in Max was visible. He seemed less stressed, more energetic, and importantly, happier. His work continued to thrive, but now it was complemented by a well-rounded personal life.

Reflection Point: How balanced is your life currently? Are there areas where you're giving too much or too little attention? What steps can you take to create a better balance?

Let's take a 'Coffee Break':

Sweet Life Lessons Exercise:

- ✓ Write down three recent highs and lows in your life. Next to each, jot down what you learned from the experience.
- ✓ Take a look at your current lifestyle. Identify areas where imbalance exists.
- ✓ For each area of imbalance, list down actions you can take to restore balance.

Just like the harmonious mix of hot espresso and cold ice cream in an Affogato, life is a blend of highs and lows of effort and ease. Embracing this balance with acceptance and resilience makes the journey not just bearable but enjoyable.

Part 7

Global Symphony of Flavors: Exploring Coffees from Around the World

As we wrap up our coffee-inspired journey, remember that just like making the perfect coffee, there's no one-size-fits-all approach to life. The beauty lies in experimenting, learning, and finding what works best for you. Cheers to brewing a life that's as unique and flavorful as your favorite cup of coffee! This part talks about my experiences with different unique coffee styles from around the world. As an avid coffee enthusiast, every time I would travel to a different part of the world, I would make it a point to taste unique coffees from various corners of the globe. Each cup offered a glimpse into a different culture, a story of tradition and craftsmanship. Let me share a few compositions of these remarkable brews and the valuable life lessons they impart.

- Kopi Luwak (Indonesia): This rare and controversial coffee is made from beans that have undergone a fascinating journey through the digestive system of civet cats. As I savored its smooth and earthy flavor, I realized the lesson of embracing unconventional paths. Kopi Luwak reminded me that sometimes, the most extraordinary experiences come from stepping outside the ordinary and exploring uncharted territories.

- Yemeni Mocha (Yemen): A sip of Yemeni Mocha transported me back in time to the birthplace of coffee itself. Its rich, wine-like acidity and complex flavors spoke of a heritage steeped in tradition. From this cup, I drew the lesson of celebrating our roots. Just as this ancient variety honors its Yemeni heritage, we should embrace our own origins, cultures, and histories, for they shape our identities and provide a strong foundation.

- Geisha Coffee (Panama): The ethereal Geisha coffee dazzled my taste buds with its delicate floral and fruity notes. This exceptional brew taught me the value of pursuing excellence. Like the meticulous cultivation and meticulous preparation of Geisha beans, our journey in life calls for continuous refinement, dedication, and striving for greatness in everything we do.

- Turkish Coffee (Turkey): Thanks to my friends, I got to taste authentic Turkish coffee. The aromatic fragrance of Turkish coffee, brewed in a cezve and served in elegant cups, spoke of a rich cultural tradition. Sipping this velvety unfiltered brew encouraged me to savor life's simple pleasures. Turkish coffee reminded me to slow down, be present at the moment, and find joy in the small and meaningful aspects of everyday life.

- Egg Coffee (Vietnam): The unique combination of Vietnamese coffee, egg yolks, and sweetened condensed milk in Egg Coffee intrigued me. Its creamy and sweet flavor profile inspired me to embrace fusion and creativity. Just as this blend brought together unexpected elements to create something delightful, we should fearlessly explore diverse ideas, blend different perspectives, and unleash our creativity to forge new paths and experiences.

From these global coffee adventures, I learned that life is a symphony of flavors, cultures, and experiences. It presents us with diverse compositions, just like the coffees from around the world. Each brew and its story teach us valuable lessons: to embrace the unconventional, celebrate our heritage, pursue excellence, savor simplicity, and foster creativity.

By embracing these lessons, we can navigate life's challenges with a sense of adventure, appreciate the richness of our experiences, and find joy in the delightful blend of flavors life offers. So, let us raise our cups and toast to the diverse and inspiring coffees from around the world, and the profound lessons they bring to our lives.

THE FINAL SIP: MASTERING THE ART

As the last notes of the coffee symphony reach our lips, we find ourselves at the end of this fascinating exploration of life, filtered through the vibrant, diverse universe of coffee. We've embarked on a flavorful journey together, navigating the parallels and intersections between coffee and life, each with their intricate dance of flavors, aromas, and experiences.

Through each cup of coffee, we've discovered and explored different facets of life - the potent Espresso mirroring resilience and strength, the versatile Americano echoing adaptability and flexibility, the layered Macchiato resonating with the complexities and subtleties of life's experiences, the balanced Cappuccino embodying harmony, the nuanced Latte representing the importance of perspective, the sweet Affogato, a reminder to cherish life's joyful moments, and the bittersweet Irish Coffee serving as a testament to life's contrasting tastes. Each coffee has enriched our understanding of life and its dynamic rhythm, illustrating the diversity of our experiences and emphasizing the importance of savoring them all.

Several years ago, I found myself walking down the familiar lanes of my childhood town. As I tread along the cobbled streets and rustic homes, a rush of nostalgia swept over me. The most palpable was the memory of my old tuition teacher's house, a place that held witness to my foundational lessons in discipline, commitment, and growth. This detour into the past served as a potent reminder of how life, much like coffee, is less about attaining perfection and more about embracing the process and enjoying the journey.

Each individual's path in life is as unique as their preferred cup of coffee. There's no universal right or wrong way of living, only a multitude of paths, each offering different experiences and insights. What truly counts is identifying the path that resonates with your values, desires, and dreams and having the courage to stay on it while constantly evolving, adapting, and growing.

It's intriguing how certain interactions etch themselves into our hearts and minds. An unforgettable encounter for me was with Mrs. Tan in Manila. Her powerful narration of the 'crab mentality' story left an indelible mark on me, ingraining a valuable lesson in me to uplift others rather than pull them down. This principle has been an illuminating beacon guiding me through life's myriad pathways.

As we come to the conclusion of this flavorful journey, I hope that it serves not to reshape you into someone new but to facilitate your evolution into the most exceptional version of yourself. It's about cultivating change, embracing growth opportunities, and wholeheartedly participating in the grand voyage; that is life.

As we bid adieu, I hope that each subsequent sip of coffee you savor will serve as a gentle nudge, reminding you of your boundless potential and the transformative lessons we've shared. Just as each fresh cup of coffee offers a chance to rejuvenate and refocus, so does each new day of life.

The words of renowned coffee connoisseur, Howard Schultz, elegantly encapsulate this sentiment, "We are not in the coffee business serving people, but in the people business serving coffee." Similarly, this book is more than just life lessons with a coffee motif. It's an endeavor to enrich your life, to serve you wisdom and insights steeped in the essence of coffee, one cup at a time.

So here's to life! A toast to resilience, adaptability, perpetual learning, balance, joy, and an indomitable spirit. To live passionately, savoring every sip of life, every moment, every experience. To your journey, may it be as robust, vibrant, and fulfilling as the most exquisite coffee. Cheers!

www.ingramcontent.com/pod-product-compliance
Ingram Content Group UK Ltd.
Pitfield, Milton Keynes, MK11 3LW, UK
UKHW062305290726
14090UKWH00018B/899

9 789356 217447